SCULPTING SHADOWS

SOHINI SINHA

Made with ♥ on the Notion Press Platform
www.notionpress.com

To every teenager standing at the crossroads of life—

This book is for you. For the dreamers and the doubters, the rebels and the quiet souls, the ones who feel lost and the ones still searching. "Sculpting Shadows" is a reflection of the joys, struggles, heartbreaks, and triumphs that shape the teenage years.

May these words remind you that you are not alone, that your feelings are valid, and that even in the chaos, you are sculpting yourself into something strong, beautiful, and whole.

With love and understanding,
Sohini Sinha

Contents

Contents

Preface

Teenage years are often described as the most vibrant yet the most chaotic chapter of life. It is a time of firsts—first love, first heartbreak, first taste of independence, and first encounters with the harsh realities of the world. It's an age of self-exploration, of questioning everything, of feeling both invincible and invisible at the same time.

"Sculpting Shadows" was born from the emotions, struggles, and silent battles that define this stage of life. Each poem in this collection captures the raw essence of being a teenager—navigating friendships, heartbreak, dreams, insecurities, and the constant tug-of-war between fitting in and standing out.

This book is not just a collection of words; it is a space where emotions find a voice, where struggles feel understood, and where readers can see themselves reflected in its pages. My hope is that every teenager who picks up this book feels a little less alone, a little more seen, and a little more empowered to embrace their journey—sculpting themselves into who they are meant to be.

To those who have outgrown their teenage years, may this book take you back, reminding you of the fire, the fragility, and the resilience of youth.

With heart and honesty,

Sohini Sinha

Acknowledgements

"Sculpting Shadows" is more than just a collection of poetry, it is a heartfelt reflection of the emotions, struggles, and experiences that shape teenage life. This book would not have been possible without the love, support, and inspiration from so many people, and I am deeply grateful to each one of them.

First and foremost, I want to thank my family for their unwavering belief in me, even when I doubted myself. Your support has been my greatest strength.

To my friends, who have been my safe space and my greatest inspiration—you have filled my life with laughter, lessons, and countless unforgettable moments that have found their way into these pages.

To every teenager out there who has ever felt lost, unheard, or misunderstood—this book is for you. Your struggles, dreams, and resilience are what inspired me to write, and I hope these words bring you comfort and courage.

Lastly, to every reader who takes the time to dive into this book, thank you. Your presence in these pages gives them meaning, and I hope "Sculpting Shadows" resonates with you in the way it was meant to.

Prologue

Shadows are more than just the absence of light, they are the echoes of who we are, the parts of ourselves we often keep hidden. Growing up, we find ourselves sculpting these shadows—shaping our fears, our dreams, our regrets, and our hopes into something we can understand, something we can live with.

Teenage years are filled with contradictions—feeling lost yet wanting to be found, craving freedom while fearing the unknown, searching for love but running from pain. It is in these moments, in the quiet struggles and unspoken emotions, that we begin to mold ourselves.

"Sculpting Shadows" is a journey through the heart of adolescence—the joy, the heartbreak, the loneliness, and the self-discovery. Each poem is a reflection of the battles fought in silence, the weight of expectations, the beauty of fleeting moments, and the strength it takes to carve your own path.

This book is for those who have ever felt like they are standing between light and darkness, unsure of which way to go. May these words remind you that even shadows are proof of the light that exists within you.

1. The White Coat Dream

Under the weight of notes and books,
Sleepless nights and anxious looks,
A NEET aspirant's fight is long,
But her parents' faith keeps her strong.
From biology charts to chemistry laws,
She scribbles answers, with barely a pause.
Physics problems, her greatest test,
Yet she pushes on, giving her best.
Her parents toil through every day,
Their sacrifices light her way.
When giving up feels far too near,
Their tired smiles dissolve her fear.
For the white coat dream, she'll strive and strive,
To make their hopes come alive.
One exam, one chance, one goal in sight,
She'll make it through, their beacon of light.

2. Shadows Forged In Silence

In quiet corners of her mind,
She gathers pieces, hard to find,
Like shattered glass, reflections blurred,
The world too loud, her thoughts unheard.
A whisper echoes through her heart,
But no one listens, torn apart,
Her voice is swallowed, lost in air—
A storm of questions everywhere.
The weight of growing up feels tight,
Like chains that bind her through the night,
The future's glare, a cruel light,
Her path unclear, no end in sight.
She wears a smile, soft and shy,
But behind it, shadows lie,
Forged in silence, tempered deep,
A girl whose secrets never sleep.
The world asks, What do you want to be?
But she's lost in her own plea,
Where dreams once soared, now fall in shame,
And she wonders if she's just a name.

Each step is heavy, each breath unsure,
Caught in the tide, so hard, so pure,
But somewhere in the silence, a spark remains—
A whisper of courage, hidden in chains.
For shadows, though dark, can lead to light,
Forged in the quiet, carved in the night.
And though she may wander, unsure, unsteady,
The girl she will be is slowly ready.

3. Chaos Of Growing-Up

At seventeen, I stand on the edge,
Between childhood's fade and adulthood's pledge,
In a world that expects me to be wise,
While my innocence fades with each passing sigh.
The streets are crowded, my heart is still,
But the eyes that follow, they never chill.
A glance, a whisper, a touch uncalled,
In the silence of the night, my soul is appalled.
I wear the mask of confidence well,
But inside, there's a storm I can't quell.
I want to speak, to shout, to fight,
But society's rules silence my might.
Boys and men, they roam with ease,
While I'm bound by judgments, trapped in their tease.
My body is mine, but they claim it still,
A victim of their gaze, against my will.
I'm told to be careful, to walk the line,
That my reputation is fragile, fine.
But why am I the one who must protect,
When they're the ones who fail to respect?
In school, at home, the pressure's the same,
To be quiet, to smile, to play the game.

I'm taught to be soft, to never be loud,
To bow my head and blend with the crowd.
But inside, there's fire, there's rage, there's fight,
I'm tired of the whispers that pierce the night.
I'm tired of the rules that cage me tight,
Of the shame they place on my body, my right.
I'm seventeen, not a child anymore,
But in the eyes of society, I'm always unsure.
Expected to be perfect, poised, and bright,
But I'm still just trying to make it through the night.
For every woman, for every girl,
The chaos of growing up swirls and twirls,
In a world that asks us to be both kind and tough,
While we endure the battle of "enough is enough."

4. Sculpting Trust

We met like sparks in summer skies,
Laughter loud, dreams held high.
Hand in hand, through highs and lows,
A bond unshaken—so it goes.
Late-night talks and endless calls,
Secrets whispered, breaking walls.
Through every twist, every fight,
We stayed strong, held on tight.
Like a ride that loops and sways,
We spun through joy, we lost our way.
But then one day, without a sound,
You chose new hands, left me unbound.
No goodbye, no second glance,
Just fading footsteps, lost in chance.
Was it real, or just pretend?
Or were we strangers in the end?
The ride has stopped, the seats are bare,
I sit alone, but I don't despair.
For though you left, I've come to see—
Some friendships fade, but I am free.

5. The Shattered Vow

I gave you my trust, a fragile thing,
A gift so pure, without a string.
I spoke of fears I dared not face,
Laid bare my soul in a sacred space.
With trembling voice, I shared it all,
Every crack, each rise, each fall.
I believed you'd hold my secrets tight,
Shield them gently, out of sight.
But you, the keeper, broke the vow,
And all my truths lie scattered now.
You whispered words to eager ears,
Unveiling my heart, exposing my fears.
Now I stand, ashamed, betrayed,
Haunted by the trust I laid.
My insecurities, my hidden pain,
Turned to whispers in a cruel refrain.
I blame myself for being blind,
For placing faith where none aligned.
How foolish was I to think you'd care,
To hope my burdens you'd humbly bear?
The shame is heavy; it pulls me down,
I wear it now, a thorny crown.

Yet in this darkness, a spark appears—
A lesson carved from all these tears.
The fault's not mine for being true,
For sharing wounds and trusting you.
The shame belongs to those who break,
The trust that others bravely make.
So though I grieve, I will not fall,
For truth and trust are worth it all.
And someday, when the pain will pass,
I'll trust again—though less, perhaps.

6. Perfection's Prison

They say, "Be bold, be strong, stand tall,"
Yet whisper, "Don't you dare to fall."
A silent script, a hidden rule—
Perfection's throne inside the school.
A flawless face, a measured smile,
A perfect grade, a trend, a style.
They chase the image, chase the dream,
But crack beneath the polished gleam.
She counts the likes, the hearts, the views,
A silent war she's set to lose.
He hides his fears behind a grin,
Afraid the world might see within.
They paint their lives in shades unreal,
Suppress the weight they truly feel.
A burden built with quiet hands,
Of expectations, strict demands.
Yet in the cracks, the truth still glows—
Perfection's just a lie they chose.
For hearts are wild, and souls are free,
Not made for cages—let them be.

7. Chasing Dreams, Carrying Doubts

In shadows cast by youthful light,
They dream of days just out of sight,
A battlefield within their chest,
Of futures calling, hearts unrest.
Her eyes chase skies too far to hold,
A world of stories yet untold.
She longs to rise, to carve her place,
Yet fears the weight she'll one day face.
He stands where crossroads twist and weave,
With dreams too wild to yet believe.
A silent vow within his mind,
To break the chains he's yet to find.
They fight the doubts that haunt their sleep,
The whispered burdens buried deep.
Will they become what they pursue?
Or will the world reshape them too?
The clock is loud, the years so fast,
They cling to moments meant to last.
Unspoken battles, hearts unseen,
Between the fear and what could be.

Yet still they dream through endless nights,
Their fragile hopes like rising lights.
For in the storm, their hearts will learn—
To shape the lives for which they yearn.

8. The Road Ahead

The clock keeps ticking, the days rush past,
Yet I stand still, afraid to ask—
What waits beyond this fleeting now?
What if I fail? What if I drown?
Dreams feel heavy, paths unclear,
A war between hope and fear.
"What will you be?" they always say,
But what if I don't find my way?
The future looms, vast and wide,
A road unknown, no map to guide.
I chase the stars, yet fear the fall,
What if I'm nothing at all?
But fear is loud, and still, I rise,
For every dawn lights up the skies.
Step by step, I'll walk, I'll try,
The future's mine—I won't deny.

9. Broken Illusion

I dream in colors, bright and wild,
A world where I am free, a child.
No limits, no fears, no rules to bind,
Just endless skies and peace of mind.
But morning comes, the world is loud,
Reality wears a heavy shroud.
Grades, expectations, futures planned,
Dreams slip like grains of sand.
"Follow your heart," they always say,
Then hand me maps, show me the way.
But what if I don't want that path?
What if I chase, what if I crash?
Between what is and what could be,
A battle rages deep in me.
Yet maybe both can find their place—
A dreamer strong enough to face.

10. Filtered Reality

Scrolling, tapping, day and night,
Chasing lives bathed in perfect light.
Filtered smiles, flawless skin,
A race I run but never win.
They have the looks, the fame, the glow,
While I stand still, stuck below.
Numbers rule, likes define,
Am I enough, or just online?
Lost in screens, I lose my face,
A stranger trapped in endless chase.
Yet beyond the glass, the real me waits,
Far from the noise, beyond the fates.
So I pause, I breathe, I see the sky,
A world untouched, where I can fly.
Not by trends, nor fleeting fame,
But by the spark within my name.

11. Choice Between Shadow & Light

They say, "Blend in, don't be too loud,"
"Follow the rules, stay with the crowd."
So I shape myself to fit the mold,
Hiding the parts that feel too bold.
I wear the trends, I speak the same,
A shadow lost inside the game.
But in the mirror, eyes ask why—
Is this me, or just a lie?
Yet standing out feels just as tough,
Being different is never enough.
Whispers trail, stares burn deep,
"Why can't you just fit in and keep?"
So I walk a line, thin as air,
Between wanting to stand, yet needing to pair.
But maybe "fitting" isn't the key—
Maybe the best thing is just to be me

12. Echoes Of Freedom

Seventeen, caught in a storm,
Between old ways and a world unborn.
Feet that ache to run so far,
Hands still bound by unseen bars.
They say, "Beta, wait your turn,"
But inside, my fire burns.
Dreams don't fit in silver plates,
Nor in rules or locked-up gates.
The streets hum songs of endless flight,
Neon dreams and city lights.
Yet voices whisper, "Think of pride,"
"Girls don't roam, boys abide."
I crave the sky, the untamed air,
A life beyond this guarded stare.
Not just duties, not just fears,
Not a road paved with silent tears.
Let me stumble, let me fall,
Let me answer my own call.
For freedom isn't just a dream—
It's the right to choose, to truly be.

13. The Space Between Us

Family—where love is meant to stay,
Yet some words slip, fade away.
I speak my heart, they hear it wrong,
A silent war we've fought too long.
"You're too young, you wouldn't know,"
"Life will teach you as you grow."
But in their eyes, they fail to see,
The storm of thoughts inside of me.
Rules like chains, concern too tight,
Why must love feel like a fight?
I pull away, they hold me near,
Bound by love, yet lost in fear.
Still, in the silence, love remains,
Through every tear, through all the pain.
Misunderstood, yet still we stay,
Love speaks loud in its own way.

14. In The Silence Of Sacrifiece

I should understand him—
his wounds, his fears, his pain.
I should be patient, forgiving,
and bear the weight again.
But what about me?
What about the nights I break,
silencing my own heart's cries
for a love that feels like take?
What about my trust,
fractured time and time before?
Yet he dares to question me
as if I'm the one unsure.
Why must I be the one to bend,
to bleed so love survives?
Why is my heart an afterthought
while he keeps his guarded tight?
I should understand him—
but who will understand me?
Because love should never cost my soul,
and I deserve to be free.

15. Scars Of Solitude

In love's aftermath, a silent storm,
Heartbreak's chill, a lonesome form.
His footsteps fade, no more texts,
One-sided love is a lingering pain.
In solitude, she learns to cope,
A canvas blank, devoid of hope.
She wears a smile, a fragile guise,
Hiding tears behind her eyes.
Memories linger, a tender scar,
She'll heal in time, near or far.
One-sided love, a bittersweet song,
In solitude, she'll find she's strong.

16. Trapped Twilight Thought

The clock blinks past 2 AM,
Eyes wide, lost in the mayhem.
Thoughts swirl, a tangled thread,
Echoes of words left unsaid.
Did I laugh too loud today?
Did they mean it when they stayed?
What if I'm just a passing phase,
A name forgotten in their days?
Dreams and fears collide in waves,
Future calls, but doubt enslaves.
What if I fail? What if I fall?
What if I never find it all?
Moonlight spills across my skin,
A war outside, a war within.
Morning waits, but I just lay,
Drowning in things I'll never say.

17. Barely Breathing

The villain in your story,
The shadow you curse when the sun slips away.
The bitter taste in the back of your throat,
The stormcloud that turns every blue to gray.
You see me as poison,
But I was once pure.
Now I'm tangled in barbs,
Too fractured for a cure.
I've thought of ending it all,
Letting the darkness devour the light.
But some cruel instinct keeps pulling me forward,
Though each breath feels like a fight.
I drag my feet through days that never end,
Existing more out of spite than hope.
Every heartbeat feels borrowed,
Every thought a knotted rope.
I wonder if they know,
If they see the cracks beneath the mask.
Or if they've all just grown tired
Of asking questions I can't unmask.
The mirror whispers, "You're the problem."
The world nods, as if it knew.

I wish I could argue,
But deep down, I think it's true.
Still, I survive, though I barely know why,
Clinging to threads of a life half-lived.
Even as guilt and grief consume me,
Even as I have nothing left to give.
Maybe this is my punishment:
To wander through shadows, unloved and alone.
A villain in your story,
A stranger to my own.

18. The Shadow They Name Too Soon

They call it depression, a heavy word,
Worn too quickly, misunderstood, unheard.
A fleeting cloud, a passing rain,
Mistaken for storms of endless pain.
For true depression is a silent tide,
An anchor that drags, a shadow that hides.
It lingers, it drains, it seeps in slow,
A thief of joy, a steady foe.
Yet teenagers grasp at fleeting woe,
Labeling moments they barely know.
A failed exam, a harsh word said,
A restless night, thoughts in their head.
Stress and anxiety knock on the door,
Born of pressure, trust lost, and more.
Friendships crumble, insecurities swell,
In the maze of youth, it's hard to tell.
But stress is a whisper, a fleeting call,
Anxiety a wave that may rise and fall.
Depression's weight, though, is heavy and vast,
A battle that grips, a shadow that lasts.

Oh, dear youth, pause, reflect, and see,
Your struggles are valid, your pain is key.
But know the name for the burden you bear,
For misnaming the weight won't lift the despair.
Speak your truth, but seek to discern,
The lessons within, the paths to learn.
Stress and anxiety may fade with care,
Depression's abyss needs more repair.
Reach out for help, don't face it alone,
In the hands of love, true strength is shown.
For every label carries its weight,
Know the journey, don't misname your state.

19. Scars To Strength

The past still lingers, soft yet loud,
A shadow woven in every cloud.
Memories play like old, worn songs,
A loop of what went right—and wrong.
The words I wish I didn't say,
The nights that stole my light away.
Faces gone, yet still so near,
Echoes trapped in silent fear.
But holding on won't change the past,
The clock moves forward, never back.
So I breathe, I stand, I take my time,
Not every scar still has to shine.
The past is part of who I am,
Yet it won't shape my final plan.
With every step, with every breath,
I let go—and live instead.

20. Finding Myself

Not the thinnest, not the best,
Not like the girls who ace the test.
Not the fastest, not the strong,
Not the one who "belongs."
I've heard the whispers, seen the stares,
Felt the weight of silent glares.
Tried to change, to shrink, to hide,
Fought a war against my pride.
But in the mirror, day by day,
I see a girl who's here to stay.
Not perfect—no, but strong and free,
And that's enough, enough for me.
I am laughter, I am light,
I am courage, fire, fight.
And though the world may not yet see,
I'm finding love inside of me.

Un-noticed Magic

Not every spark lights up the sky,
Not every laugh is loud and high.
But in the quiet, in between,
Magic lives—though often unseen.
    A baby's hand wrapped tight in yours,
A sunset glow through open doors.
The smell of rain, the warmth of tea,
A song that brings back memories.
    A friend who stays when times are tough,
A stranger's smile—sometimes enough.
The hush of dawn, the moon's soft gleam,
The joy of chasing half-lost dreams.
    Life rushes fast, the years unwind,
But look around, and you will find—
The biggest joys, the love so true,
Live in the moments that slip right through.

To My Readers

Each word I write, each verse I weave,
Finds its meaning when you believe.
These pages hold my heart and mind,
Yet in your hands, they come alive.

You've walked these lines, felt the pain,
Danced in sunshine, cried in rain.
With every whisper, every sigh,
You've seen the world through my eyes.

For every moment you took to read,
For finding solace when you need,
For letting my words touch your soul,
You made this journey feel whole.

So here's my thanks, deep and true,
This book exists because of you.
May you always find, in words or light,
A piece of hope to hold on tight.

www.ingramcontent.com/pod-product-compliance
Lightning Source LLC
LaVergne TN
LVHW091242150826
845673LV00003B/1250

* 9 7 9 8 8 9 7 4 4 3 9 9 4 *